The Forerunners

The Forerunners
Black Poets in America

edited by WOODIE KING, JR.

With an introduction by Addison Gayle, Jr.
and a preface by Dudley Randall

HOWARD UNIVERSITY PRESS WASHINGTON, D.C. 1975

Printed in the United States of America

Library of Congress Cataloging in Publication Data

King, Woodie, comp.
  The forerunners.

  CONTENTS: Samuel Allen.—Russell Atkins.—Arna
Bontemps. [etc.]
  1. American poetry—Negro authors. 2. American
poetry—20th century. I. Title.
PS591.N4K5   811'.5'08   74-31169
ISBN 0-88258-015-9

Grateful acknowledgments are made to the following:

Samuel Allen for permission to reprint "My Friend" by Samuel Allen from *Nommo* by William Robinson, Macmillan 1972. Copyright © 1972 by Samuel Allen; and for "Nat Turner" by Samuel Allen from *Black Writers of America* by Barksdale and Kinnamon, Macmillan 1972. Copyright © 1972 by Samuel Allen.

Russell Atkins for permission to reprint "Probability and Birds in the Yard" from *Poetry: Cleveland.* Copyright © 1971 by Cleveland State University Poetry Center; "New Storefront" from *Hearse Magazine.* Copyright © 1972 by Hearse Press; and for permission to print "Dark Area" by Russell Atkins.

Black World for permission to reprint "Ski Trail" by Samuel Allen, from *Negro Digest,* Vol, XVIII, No. 12, October 1969. Copyright © 1969 by Samuel Allen; for "At Home in Dakar" by Margaret Danner, from *Negro Digest,* Vol. XV, No. 9, July 1966. Copyright © 1966 by *Negro Digest;* and for "A Grandson is a Hoticeberg" by Margaret Danner, from *Black World,* Vol. XX, No. 11, September 1971. Copyright © 1971 by *Black World.*

Broadside Press for permission to reprint "The Life of Lincoln West" and "Estimable Mable" from *Family Pictures* by Gwendolyn Brooks. Copyright © 1970 by Gwendolyn Brooks Blakely; for "Black Soul of the Land" by Lance Jeffers from *My Blackness Is the Beauty of This Land* by Lance Jeffers. Copyright © 1970 by Lance Jeffers; for "Trellie" by Lance Jeffers from *When I Know the Power of My Black Hand* by Lance Jeffers. Copyright © 1972, 1974 by Lance Jeffers; for "Green Apples" by Dudley Randall from *Broadside,* No. 62. Copyright © 1972 by Dudley Randall; and for "Ballad of the Hoppy-Toad" and "Jackson, Mississippi" by Margaret Walker from *Prophets for a New Day* by Margaret Walker. Copyright © 1970 by Margaret Walker.

Sterling A. Brown for permission to reprint "Slim in Hell," "Southern Road," "Old Lem," and "Strong Men" by Sterling A. Brown, and also for an excerpt from *Negro Poetry and Drama* by Sterling A. Brown.

Margaret Burroughs for permission to print "Everybody But Me" by Margaret Burroughs.

Margaret Danner for permission to print "The Rhetoric of Langston Hughes" by Margaret Danner.

Frank Marshall Davis for permission to reprint "To Those Who Sing America," "Dancing Gal," and "Onward Christian Soldiers!" by Frank Marshall Davis.

Owen Dodson for permission to print "The Morning Duke Ellington Praised the Lord and Six Little Black Davids Tapped Danced Unto," "Ballad of Badmen," and "Job's Ancient Lament" by Owen Dodson.

Robert Hayden for permission to reprint "Richard Hunt's Arachne," "The Night-Blooming Cereus," and "The Peacock Room" from *The Night-Blooming Cereus* by Robert Hayden. Copyright © 1972 by Robert Hayden.

Percy Johnston for permission to reprint "Love Pictures You as

To the memory
of Langston Hughes

Preface

O ne of the first projects of Howard University Press was the presentation of a festival of black poets entitled "Forerunners." It took place on Howard's campus and was co-produced by Woodie King. The title reflected the program's focus on those poets who were a bridge between generations—lyricists who carried the baton of poetic tradition from the Renaissance into the forties and fifties, and created the foundation for the writers of the sixties and seventies.

The festival was aptly dedicated to Langston Hughes, and the poets read a poem of the beloved poet or reminisced about how Hughes had so unselfishly helped them. Because of their mutual and emotional link with him, a special air permeated the readings. There were particularly poignant moments when Owen Dodson, recently operated on, read his poems from a wheelchair, and when the revered Sterling Brown read "Strong Men" with tears in his eyes.

Now Howard University Press has published an anthology of the festival, containing a selection of the poems read there. The poems contained here are not only those written during the forties and fifties, but include some more recent ones, which indicate that the poets are still productive and creative. This anthology is further enriched by statements from the poets about the future of their craft in a sometimes unpoetic world and about themselves as poets.

Dudley Randall

Contents

Introduction

BY ADDISON GAYLE, JR.

In too many instances, black writers in America have written in response to outside pressures, have attempted to create a literature in accordance with the actions or reactions of a white majority. For this reason, it is not too far wrong to suggest that until quite recently theirs has been a literature of reaction. Richard Wright was among the first to note this tendency, and in the essay "The Literature of the Negro in the United States" he traces the history of black poetry from Phillis Wheatley to Margaret Walker and concludes that a trend away from "strictly racial themes," as shown in the works of many poets, was due to improvement in the condition of black people. If the literature of the future, he warned, returns to preoccupation with racial themes, this will indicate that Blacks "are suffering . . . old and ancient agonies at the hands of our white American neighbors." Conversely, continuation of a literature that assumes ". . . the common themes and burdens of literary expression, which are the heritage of all men," means that "a humane attitude prevails in America towards us [Blacks]."

Two major tendencies distinguished the literature of reaction. First, it was a service literature, offered as evidence that Blacks were not an inferior people, and regarded by many practitioners—James Weldon Johnson, Jessie R. Fauset, and Angelina W. Grimké come readily to mind—as an instrument designed to articulate the grievances of the black middle class. Second, it was viewed by some as an instrument of catharsis, the vehicle to produce an awareness of the crippling effects of "our old and ancient agonies" in the minds of "our white neighbors." The practitioners, which include Wright and the school of protest writers he inspired, believed that literature could produce changes in the attitudes of whites sufficient to cause positive changes in the black condition.

Belief in the possibility of American redemption is central to the proponents of each position. Even the most militant —and Claude McKay is a good example—appealed to America and, in so doing, often ignored the varied dimensions of the black experience. In making the argument for tolerance and consideration, too many black writers, then and now, exaggerated the conditions of their black subjects and, in many cases, accepted arguments based upon black inferiority and white superiority. Such characteristics are endemic to black writing as a whole; yet they are nowhere more discerning than in the area of black poetry. The first recognized black poet in America, Jupiter Hammon, gives thanks to God and white men alike, in stilted eighteenth-century diction, for rescuing him from supposed barbarism:

> O come you pious youth! Adore
> The wisdom of thy God
> In bringing thee from distant shore
> To learn his holy word.

> Thou mightst been left behind,
> Amidst a dark abode;
> God's tender mercy still combin'd,
> Thou hast the holy word.

Wheatley, the first American woman poet of renown, copies Hammon's sentiments, while improving upon his poetry:

> 'Twas not long since I left my native shore,
> The land of errors and Egyptian gloom:

> Father of mercy! 'twas thy gracious hand
> Brought me in safety from those dark abodes.

Lester P. Hill, a poet of another age and time, uses the couplet form to convince his "white neighbors" of the continual devotion of Blacks, despite their ordeal:

> We will not waver in our loyalty.
> No strange voice reaches us across the sea:
> No crime at home shall stir us from his soil.
> Ours is the guerdon, ours the blight of toil,
> But raised above it by a faith sublime
> We choose to-suffer here and bide our time.

Appeals to whites, and catalogues of our ancient agonies, also form the unifying theme of militant poetry. "Throw the children into the river," writes Fenton Johnson, "civilization has given us too many/It is better to die than to grow up and find that you are colored." Lines from McKay's sonnet make the point more strongly:

> Your door is shut against my tightened face,
> And I am sharp as steel with discontent;
> But I possess the courage and the grace
> To bear my anger proudly and unbent.

The eternal note of black despair is voiced even during the period of Black Power and black revolt. Carl Wendell Himes, Jr., writes:

> there he stands. see?
> like a black Ancient Mariner his
> wrinkled old face so
> full of the wearies of living is
> turned downward with
> closed eyes. his frayed-collar
> faded-blue old shirt turns

dark with sweat & the old
necktie undone drops
loosely about the worn
old jacket see? . . .

There are few models for such poets in the history of the
Western world. They are descendants of those who underwent
cultural shock, who were separated by brutal wrenching from
one culture and denied the right to immerse themselves com-
pletely in another. Though the separation from the old culture
was not complete—vestiges remained in the animal tales, in
some lines from the spirituals, in ditties and anecdotes, and in
certain religious practices—still, the Africa of their fathers,
seat of the culture which had nourished a race, was deemed
inferior by the most eminent of Western scholars. The reaction
of Blacks in general and black poets in particular was to
search for a sense of identity, of cultural security in a hostile
and strange environment.

Disassociated from one culture and denied entrance into
another, they were torn between love and hate toward the
land that had enslaved their fathers. This accounts for the
ambiguity of much of their verse, for the simultaneous out-
pouring of anger and hope. There is anger in the poetry of
James M. Whitfield:

America, it is to thee,
Thou boasted land of liberty—
It is to thee that I raise my song,
Thou land of blood, and crime, and wrong,
It is to thee my native land,
     From which has issued many a band
To tear the black man from his soil
And force him here to delve and toil
Chained on your blood-bemoistened sod,
Cringing beneath a tyrant's rod . . .

There is hope in the despondent appeal of Langston Hughes:

> Let America be America again,
> Let it be the dream it used to be.
> Let it be the pioneer on the plain.
> Seeking a home where he himself is free.

> (America never was America to me.)

The single line refrain intruded into the format of the poem does not obviate the poet's desire to be one with the culture that denies him, or his wish to redeem the America that "lies deep in the heart of me." Whitfield and Hughes are examples of black poets prevented by a love-hate relationship with America from recognizing (or admitting) its true nature. Neither could accept the fact that the culture upon which they had been so "crudely grafted" offered no sanctuary, would force them, in time, to seek to step outside even the cultural no man's land into which it had consigned them. We are not nationalists because of the devil, writes Imamu Baraka, we would be nationalists if no devil ever existed. Those not able to articulate their grievances in such terminology, nevertheless, when forced finally to confront reality, would be forced also to renounce the dream of "an America yet to be!"

The poetry written before such an epiphany, however, is a romantic poetry, oftentimes evidencing nothing so much as the poets' ignorance of the facts of history. Therefore, at one and the same time, black poets pointed out some of the realities of the world in which they lived, while, in the dénouement of either singular poems or volumes, they prophesied a Canaan to be, an America redeemed and born anew. Look into the poetry of such romantics from Hammon to Hayden, and the lessons of the Middle Passage, the reality of slavery, the attempt by some men to dehumanize others, seem unlearned. Seldom do their lines vibrate with the cries and curses of those

to whom the white God never came, seldom do unnamed, un-
lettered men and women, who never dreamed the romantic
dream, appear as characters in their verse. Personages like
Harriet Tubman and Frederick Douglass appear, to be sure,
but others of lesser stature and attainments are almost always
excluded. Outside the spirituals, seldom is there displayed the
universal desire of men, not to be one with tyranny, but to
escape it, not to co-exist with evil, but to destroy it. The ex-
periences of those who passed through the nightmare of
American history have seldom been accurately recorded by
those who function as their amanuenses.

Hope, it appears, was destined to flame eternally in the
breasts of black poets. They held to optimistic views concern-
ing America even in moments of greatest anger and bitterness.
Men like W. E. B. Du Bois, capable of uttering such violent
curses as those from "A Litany of Atlanta,"—"I hate them, Oh!/
I hate them well/I hate them Christ/As I hate hell/If I were
God/I'd sound their knell/This day!"—were also capable of
sounding this hopeful chord: "If somewhere in this whirl and
chaos of things there dwells Eternal Good, pitiful yet master-
ful, then anon in His good time America shall rend the Veil
and the prisoned shall go free." This is not simply schizophre-
nia. It is, rather, an attempt by men to confront a hostile so-
ciety; it is an example of the human quality, peculiar to poets,
which causes men always to envision a world different from
the one that exists; it is the inability of men, daily under the
gun, to evaluate objectively the situation they are in.

Thus their hope and optimism is not so much misfounded
as misdirected. They were intent upon remaking America,
upon redeeming a land and people beyond redemption; there-
fore, they paid little attention to the viable culture of their
ancestors, failed to delineate the varied dimensions of black
life, wrote too few odes to nameless black heroes, and dis-
covered too little of value in the black experience. With

Wright they believed that Blacks were metaphors of the American condition; and with Wright again, they believed that Blacks, symbolizing pained and desperate men, were paradigms for men everywhere. That Blacks were metaphors of mankind in a truer, much more fundamental way escaped their imaginations. Yet the courage evidenced by those who survived the Middle Passage, by those who maintained stoic dignity and defiance in the face of oppression, denotes black people as metaphors of the universal human condition: ". . . the Negroes' most powerful images of hope and despair," wrote Wright, "still remain in the fluid state of daily speech. How many John Henrys have lived and died on the lips of Black people? How many mythical heroes in embryo have been allowed to perish for the lack of husbanding by alert intelligence?"

The answer, unfortunately, is far too many. Many black poets, in accepting the arguments of white nationalists from Thomas Jefferson to Norman Mailer that they were a people sans culture, eternal victims, mere appendages to the culture of the West, ignored the positive aspects of black life and assaulted the minds of white Americans in an attempt to validate their own humanity. Men and women who succumbed to images and symbols created by others, they seemed unable to fashion newer, more positive ones from their own experiences, were unable to resolve the dichotomy between hatred and love of America, and attempted to write, not a racial poetry, but a poetry of reaction.

For what is racial poetry? It is not merely poetry that takes as its subject matter themes and individuals of particular races. If this were so all the poetry of the Western world from *Oedipus Rex* to *The Ring and the Book* would be racial poetry. It is not poetry that merely catalogues man's suffering and travails, that denotes only his despondent condition; it is not poetry directed to those outside the race, not poetry of facile optimism, hopeless dreams, or romantic longings. Instead, racial poetry concerns itself with the varied dimensions of a people's lives, notes their strengths and weaknesses, creates new images, metaphors, and symbols from their history, and in so doing, erases the artificial line constructed by Western critics between racial and universal. Poetry which deals realistically with Blacks in America is universal in the truest sense of the term.

In the critical statements and poetry of Blacks in the sixties and seventies, there is cognition of this fact. Black art, argues Ron Karenga, must be functional, collective, and committed, must "expose the enemy, praise the people, and support the revolution. . . ." "We must," asserts Don L. Lee, "destroy Faulkner, dick, jane, and other perpetrators of evil. It's time for Du Bois, Nat Turner, and Kwame Nkrumah. . . . Black artists are cultural stabilizers; bringing back old values, and introducing new ones." Etheridge Knight is the prophet of a new world and a new poetry: "Unless the Black artist establishes a 'Black Aesthetic' he will have no future at all. To accept the white aesthetic is to accept and validate a society that will not allow him to live. The black artist must create new forms and new values, sing new songs (or purify old ones); and along with other black authorities, he must create a new history, new symbols, myths and legends (and purify old ones by fire)."

The distance in perception between the poets whom Wright discussed and those of the sixties and seventies is great indeed. The former lived and wrote before the emergence of the Black Power revolution, before the murder of Martin Luther King, before sophisticated attempts by the robot-like men of the Nixon administration to return America to ante-bellum times. They could believe, therefore, that change was possible, that the time would arrive when men would no longer be forced to create a poetry out of oppression, that America, in Hughes's words, might be America again. Their younger disciples, on the other hand, have witnessed the holocaust reborn, faced universal white resistance as they struggled for manhood rights, have known the indiscriminate murder of black people from Mississippi to New York, have borne witness to the transformation of white liberals from allies to rednecks, and have begun a movement designed to take Blacks outside American history and culture.

Through the efforts of Imamu Baraka, Askia Muhammad Touré, Don L. Lee, Sonia Sanchez, Etheridge Knight, Johari Amini, Mari Evans, Larry Neal, Willie Kgositsile, Raymond Patterson, and James Emanuel among others, a true racial poetry is being created. It is a poetry that has as its objectives the creation of a new people and a new nation and the destruction of images and symbols that enslave; it is a poetry that demands a revolution of the mind and spirit, that calls, with Baraka, for the greatest of man's creations: "We want a Black poem. And a Black world/Let the World be a Black Poem."

These young men and women are indebted to the poets of the past, to those discussed by Wright. Before they could make their presence felt among black people, the dreams held by older poets had to be sorely tested, the dichotomy between love and hate confronted and resolved, the choice made between illusion and reality, between dedication to the pragmatics of American history and continual commitment to the absurd and impossible. The perceptions of the younger poets, therefore, were sharpened by the works of their predecessors, even by the works of such poets as Hammon, Wheatley, Dunbar, and Johnson, as well as Hughes and McKay. They were sharpened and expanded, however, in a much more meaningful way by a group of poets whom editor Woodie King has labeled "the forerunners." These are the poets who came to prominence, mainly, after the Renaissance years, who bridged the gap between poets of the twenties and those of the sixties and seventies. They began the intensive questioning of the impossible dream, the final assault upon illusion that produced the confrontation with reality, the search for paradigms, images, metaphors, and symbols from the varied experiences of a people whose history stretches back beyond the Nile. With few exceptions, they are the literary godparents of today's black poets.

They are included in this volume, *The Forerunners*, and their presence makes this a unique collection of poetry, indeed. The book looks back to the past and ahead to the future. It is composed of love poetry and religious poetry, of protest poetry and poetry of resignation. There is poetry of Africa—the motherland—poetry of angst, and poetry of joy. There is angry poetry whose measured lines assault the ear and tender poetry more singsong than lyrical, which soothes and instructs as well. Most of the poems are written in blank verse, though sonnets and ballads are well represented. The editor has brought together in a single volume a variety of poems that exhibit mastery of form and content. There are the staid, timeless lines of Arna Bontemps:

> The years go back with an iron clank,
> A hand is on the gate,
> A dry leaf trembles on the wall.
> Ghosts are walking.
> They have broken roses down
> And poplars stand there still as death.

There is the questioning of Robert Hayden in the idiom peculiar to the surrealists: "Ars Longa Which is crueller/ Vita Brevis life or art?" The speaker in one of Russell Atkins's poems is nostalgic for a world outside "industries' shadows" where "(. . . sudden trees.)/flowers, a wheedle of them?/*cannabis sativa* burning/somewhere near/the volumed/

dun?" Owen Dodson forwards the black man's eternal question to his God: "God, why have you ruined me,/What have I done unto thee . . . ?" Margaret Walker implores the Old Testament God in the sentiments of the first slaves: "Pray for second sight and the inner ear. Pray for bulwark against poaching patterns of dislocated days; pray for buttressing iron against insidious termite and beetle and locust and flies and lice and moth and rust and mold."

The strength of the collection lies in its selectivity. In choosing representative poems from the works of older poets, the editor has managed to foreshadow many of the themes of today's black poets. Margaret Walker, Gwendolyn Brooks, Frank Marshall Davis, Arna Bontemps, and Sterling Brown speak with a modernity echoed in the works of their younger colleagues: Sam Allen, Lance Jeffers, Naomi Long Madgett, Dudley Randall, and Jay Wright. The themes of such poems as "A Black Man Talks of Reaping," "Dancing Gal," "Old Lem," and "At Home in Dakar" bear striking resemblance to those of such poems as "Black Soul of the Land," "Black Woman," "On Getting a Natural (For Gwendolyn Brooks)," and "My Friend." Here in one collection are the themes of love and strife between black men and women, themes which deal with the holocaust from several perspectives, images, metaphors, and symbols that depict the beauty and grandeur of a people. Lance Jeffers, one of the most talented poets represented in the volume, searches in the past for images and symbols:

> Give me your spine, old man, old man,
> give me your rugged hate,
> give me your sturdy oak-tree love,
> give me your source of steel.
> Teach me to sing so that the song may be mine
> "Keep your hands on the plow: hold on!"

One day the nation's soul shall turn black like yours
and America shall cease to be its name.

With metaphorical clarity and black insight, Gwendolyn
Brooks is at one with the poets of the seventies in her portrait
of Lincoln West, "Ugliest little boy/that everyone ever saw,"
who finds dignity and strength when realizing the uniqueness
of his color and features, when realizing that among all Blacks,
he was "the real thing." "When he was hurt, too much/stared
at—/too much/left alone—he/thought about that. He told him-
self/'After all, I'm/the real thing.' It comforted him." Like
Mari Evans and Sonia Sanchez, Naomi Long Madgett cele-
brates the beauty of black women and poses the question
sounded in their works:

> Where are my lovers?
> Where are my tall, my lovely princes
> Dancing in slow grace
> Toward knowledge of my beauty?
> Where
> Are my beautiful
> Black men?

The Forerunners has made Wright's contention in "The
Literature of the Negro in the United States" obsolete. The
continuance of oppression against Blacks by white Americans
has not caused these poets to continue the tradition begun by
their ancestors, one which resulted in a poetry of reaction.
Most of them utilize the racial idiom, and thus their poetry is
racial in the most positive sense of the term. This is due, how-
ever, not to the fact of continual oppression, but rather, to
the poets' commitment to black people, coupled with the
realization that poetry written in reaction to the whims and
fancies of other men is a facile poetry at best, one which
makes impossible the creation of positive images and symbols.

These young poets have realized that the songs of the fathers must be updated by the sons, that time and circumstances demand an ever-changing poetry. More importantly, however, they have discovered that to be universal means to step outside the parochialism of the American society, and that to be a good poet as well as a relevant poet entails as great a concern for race as it does for the mastery of craft.

It is this that distinguishes them from the earlier poets and makes them one with their younger counterparts of the sixties and seventies. Hammon, Wheatley, and Dunbar, among others, accepted all too readily the stereotypes of Blacks handed down from the Americans; they believed with their white contemporaries that Blacks were inferior, destined to be the eternal wards of superior, more human men. Their poetry is adorned with too many aunts, uncles, and mammies, too many Christ figures and apologists. Those whom Woodie King has labeled "the forerunners" have looked closely at black history and discovered truer paradigms. Such are found in the portraits of Old Lem, depicted by Sterling Brown; in the nobility and beauty of the men and women in the poetry of Naomi Long Madgett and Gwendolyn Brooks; in the digni- fied Africans who so moved Margaret Danner; in the images of courage and determination which effuse the poetry of Lance Jeffers.

These are the poets who, long before Askia Touré and Don L. Lee, recognized the most profound of truths: to con- trol the image is the responsibility of black writers, for para- digms of positive import can only be created by Blacks freed from the pretensions and hypocrisy of Western culture. They have realized that three centuries of American oppression have rendered all definitions by whites concerning Blacks irrele- vant; come to believe with Frederick Douglas that each white man is barred, due to culture and experience, from painting representative portraits of Blacks. They have realized, too, that in a country where oppression is ingrained in institutions and traditions only the insane among the oppressed are willing to accept mirror images from the oppressor.

The poets, midwifed by the Black Power revolution, are aware of such facts, and thus, they have moved to bury the contemptuous, obscene images of Blacks handed down from Western scholars, poets, and critics. They write a poetry which speaks of strong black men and women; they find positive images in the holocaust, sift through black history for monuments of a past of rebellion and revolution. Theirs is a revolutionary poetry, directing itself to black people, demanding changes in the way that Blacks perceive themselves, and calling for the construction of a new world, based upon a value system hewn out of the black experience.

Theirs is a true racial poetry, and their debt to the forerunners is great indeed. For it was these poets who broke with the tradition of the past, who dared to cross the Rubicon between acceptance by Americans and defiance of American values and customs, who dared to challenge the right assumed by the oppressor of defining the life style of the oppressed, who argued that a people with a unique history could not sing their songs in a strange and hostile land, and who urged that Blacks, writers and laymen alike, must move outside American history. Langston Hughes remains one of their patron saints; it is not, however, the Hughes of the romantic dream whom they admire, but the Hughes of *The Panther and the Lash,* who realized, finally, that salvation for Blacks is possible only through the efforts of Blacks.

Though there are those in this volume who tend to eschew race, who write a facile poetry of little meaning, who attempt to lose the black experience in abstraction and surrealism, for the most part *The Forerunners* is marked by those who have turned inward in order to better illuminate the experiences of a people. Listen to Sterling Brown in the twenties and Askia

Touré in the sixties, and note that the tradition continues un-
broken from the forerunners to their younger colleagues:

> Today they shout prohibition at you
> "Thou shalt not this"
> "Thou shalt not that"
> "Reserved for whites only"
> You laugh.
>
> One thing they cannot prohibit—
> The strong men . . . coming on
> The strong men gittin' stronger.
> Strong men . . .
> Stronger. . . .
>
> •　　•　　•
>
> In this land we will rise, we will rise
> As the pyramids of Africa rise to find the fathers of the
>   Sphinx
> We will rise as a pine tree, tall and proud, rises under
>   bloody
> Southern skies to kiss the moon
> We are the new!
> We are the rivers of the Spring breaking through
> The cold white ice of dying winter.

Words are the paper and string to package experience, to wrap up from the inside out the poet's concentric waves of contact with the living world. Each poet makes of words his own highly individualized wrappings for the segments of life he wishes to present. Sometimes the paper and string are more arresting than the contents of the package. Sometimes the poet creates a transparent wrapping revealing with great clarity and from all angles what is inside. Sometimes the word wrapping is clumsy and inept, and neither the inside nor the outside of the package is interesting. Sometimes the word wrapping contains nothing. But regardless of quality or content, a poem reveals always the poet as a person. Skilled or unskilled, wise or foolish, nobody can write a poem without revealing something of himself. Here are people. Here are poems. Here is revelation.

Sincerely,

Langston

(Note written to Russell Atkins by Langston Hughes)

· 1

SAMUEL ALLEN
[1917–]

attended Fisk University, Harvard Law School, New School for Social Research, and the Sorbonne. IIis book *Ivory Tusk* was published in 1956. Mr. Allen has contributed poetry to over fifty anthologies in America and abroad.

*I*t is evident, now, in the seventies, that black poets are continuing with an increasingly sharpened sense of direction both to define and to vivify the black experience, drawing upon and utilizing a more profoundly explored heritage. They listen with new awareness to black music, to the wisdom of the folklore, to the rhythms of the varied speech, and, like the sorcerer, conjure up from the wellsprings of the creative consciousness an identity both old and new, a vision whole and sufficient.

The black poet is decisive in the task of striking from the disparate elements of the alienated African presence in the West the coin of a new awareness. It is, indeed, a fusion which is in the process of realization, yet the emphasis is necessarily upon the denied, but essential, sources of the black experience, rather than white Western influences. We are not heirs to the Greeks, but willy-nilly we inhabit in part the cultural terrain. The poet must simultaneously discover and create his authentic voice. He must find his way in the selective use of elements from these two bodies of tradition, the resolution of which must ultimately be felt as one, which must be cast in his likeness and according to his need.

Black poetry will be, in a fuller sense, a poetry of self-discovery, of self-realization, enabling us to know and to touch the wonder and the beauty, as well as the pain, of our common lot in this time and place. It is, ultimately, in its best expression, the task of the discovery of man, not in the sense of two thousand years of a xenophobic Western culture or of some universal abstraction, but in a more humanistic celebration of our own denied and particular experience.

My Friend

I have a friend
Who reads higher mathematics and post quantum
   physics in his leisure.
He is, and has for some time been, a so-called Negro.
When he was a boy
He won a contest for the nation's high school students.
The prize was a four-year scholarship to college.
They found out he was colored
And they gave him a pin.
Even some of the Committee didn't like it
But the Daughters of the American Revolution were
   helping with the money,
And the Daughters said, unfortunately, it would offend
Our way of life.

Now my friend is not so happy with his country.
He went to a so-so school and has a so-so job
But not a so-so feeling toward his so-called country.
He laughs a fierce and high-pitched laugh
At the famed loyalty of the Negro.
I'd publish every state secret I got my hands on, he
   almost shouts.
I, of course, tell him I don't believe this
And I point out that this is unpatriotic, un-American,
   and unsafe,
And what is more, the CIA will get you if you don't—
   watch—out!
He seems to think I'm joking, laughs evil
And carries on.

His friends used to say

If Stalin were to rise from his coffin
And call for a volunteer
To lead a tank battalion through Mississippi
—there would be no problem.

Sometimes, when I see his face
At some innocent remark about the land of the free,
I recall the war photos of the Red tank commanders
Moving on Berlin . . .
I think how lucky Mississippi would be
To have THEM moving in
Instead of him . . .
My friend.

Nat Turner

From the obscurity of the past, we saw
the dark now flaming face of a giant Nathaniel
calling
whosoever will
let him come.

Turner's face softened for a moment
and he mourned for the lost years
    the eternity of grief
    the thousands, the millions of his people
    torn from the soil of their fathers
    for a living death in a strange land.

And his face hardened
and we heard, again, the voice, calling
    whosoever will
    let him come
    let him come, now
    let him come
    let him come
    let him come.

Ski Trail

Say
Did you see that magnificent blonde beast
Swooping down here aminuteago?

See who?

You know—that magnificent
                              blonde
                                    beast.
Oh him!

No . . . can't say that I have
    . . . not at all lately
    . . . not in a coon's age.

That's funny

He used to be swoopinaroundhere all—

    —of the time.

RUSSELL ATKINS
[1926–]

is a musician and a poet. His poems have appeared in various magazines since the 1940s. Recently published volumes include *Phenomena, Objects,* and *Heretofore.*

*F*or the last three decades there has been an about-face in the second half of each decade, with literary thought reflecting the changes: World War II in the first half of the forties versus "peace" in the second half; conservative academicism in the first half of the fifties versus Bohemian beatnikism in the second half; integration/Civil Rights movement in the first half of the sixties versus the separatist/militancy of the latter half.

Something similarly inverse might take place in writing in the fourth decade, during the seventies. "Black" poetry (much too "universal" seemingly—contrary to some opinion) may become more specific and varied with an accurate definition of universal; "white" poetry, which has avoided abstraction and universality (contrary to some opinion), may, in a general sense, rediscover these.

As for myself, I've a feeling that I will be in circumstances like the present one, not as much maligned, I hope, but still mustering the individual ego against inconsistency, duplication, and cliché—especially cliché.

Probability and Birds in the Yard

The probability in the yard is this:
The rodent keeps the cat close by;
The cat would sharp at the bird;
The bird would waft to the water—
if he does he has but his times before,
whichever one he is. He's surely marked.

The cat is variable;
the rodent becomes the death of the bird
which we love
         dogs are random

New Storefront

Afresh'd with paint the shop had glare:
chrome-plated the squared off for sale,
angles or with glamorous rounds.
                              Auto Supply Co.
The owner looked too outright
(dart of a much refracted stare).
Aluminum had set him blind awhile—
the false going virtue of hope

no public interest anywhere about

his innocence   among the smokeshops
the parlors of the barbeque, the bars
and barbershops proliferous. All these
dives, without sheen and more secret,
sinfully wised, merely glimmered

he dared their margins with silver

Dark Area

The thin wickedly intricate
arounded to full
and an afar haunt of fog
seemed whitely sleep.
Profanely begun
music of grass
intimately lull—

it's some murmuring dismal
stupendous'd to drear,
while the orbiting
rankled deep about
high cloud burials

There was the sidecast
of industries' shadows;
a streetlamp heaved—
I could have sworn
the stark-knuckled
held skull'd up!
(Rag shredded pike
spectreing, arched fence,
sudden trees.)

flowers, a wheedle of them?
cannabis sativa burning
        somewhere near
the volumed
dun?

ARNA BONTEMPS
[1902–1973]

was the editor of *Golden Slippers,* an anthology of Negro poetry for young people, and coeditor with Langston Hughes of *The Poetry of the Negro: 1746–1949.* His own poetry appeared in various magazines between 1924 and 1931. He was the author of a number of books for children, three novels, *God Sends Sunday, Black Thunder,* and *Drums at Dusk,* and a volume of poetry, *Personals.* IIe was also the librarian at Fisk University from 1943 to 1965.

*T*he poetry of the American Negro sometimes seems hard to pin down. Like his music, from spirituals and gospel songs to blues, jazz, and bebop, it is likely to be marked by a certain special riff, an extra glide, a kick where none is expected, and a beat for which there is no notation. It follows the literary traditions of the language it uses, but it does not hold them sacred. As a result, there has been a tendency for critics to put it in a category by itself, outside the main body of American poetry. Is American Negro poetry a part of the main-stream of American literature or isn't it?

A better way, however, might be to drop the use of main-stream as a catchword. The Negro experience in America has found a vastly satisfying medium of expression in music. If occasionally this has been felt as a mood of our time, in the broad sense, perhaps that is another matter. The lyrics of the spirituals are certainly as vital and valid as the music, and the same can be said of blues and ballads like "John Henry." From these sources comes a kind of poetic tradition, and American Negro poets have frequently associated themselves with it. However, it is well to remember that Phillis Wheatley wrote with some success before it existed, and there is certainly no way to predict what spirit will move the newest Negro poet.*

---

* *From* American Negro Poetry, *edited by Arna Bontemps*

A Black Man Talks of Reaping

I have sown beside all waters in my day.
I planted deep, within my heart the fear
That wind or fowl would take the grain away
I planted safe against this stark, lean year.

I scattered seed enough to plant the land
In rows from Canada to Mexico
But for my reaping only what the hand
Can hold at once is all that I can show.

Yet what I sowed and what the orchard yields
My brother's sons are gathering stalk and root,
Small wonder then my children glean in fields
They have not sown, and feed on bitter fruit.

Close Your Eyes!

Go through the gates with closed eyes.
Stand erect and let your black face front the west.
Drop the axe and leave the timber where it lies;
A woodman on the hill must have his rest.

Go where leaves are lying brown and wet
Forget her warm arms and her breast who mothered you,
And every face you ever loved forget.
Close your eyes; walk bravely through.

Southern Mansion

Poplars arc standing there still as death
And ghosts of dead men
Meet their ladies walking
Two by two beneath the shade
And standing on the marble steps.

There is a sound of music echoing
Through the open door
And in the field there is
Another sound tinkling in the cotton:
Chains of bondmen dragging on the ground.

The years go back with an iron clank,
A hand is on the gate,
A dry leaf trembles on the wall.
Ghosts are walking.
They have broken roses down
And poplars stand there still as death.

GWENDOLYN BROOKS
[1917–]

won a Pulitzer Prize for *Annie Allen,* and was chosen
Poet Laureate of the state of Illinois. Some of her works
include *Riot, A Street in Bronzeville, The Bean Eaters,
In the Mecca,* and *Maud Martha.* She has been awarded
two Guggenheim Fellowships, the Kuumba Liberation
Award, and has received an award from the American
Academy of Arts and Letters. Her autobiography,
Report from Part One, was published by Broadside
Press of Detroit.

I think a little more should be required of the poet than per-
haps is required of the sculptor or the painter. The poet deals
in words with which everyone is familiar. We all handle
words. And I think the poet, if he wants to speak to anyone,
is constrained to do something with those words so that they
will (I hate to use the word) mean something, will be some-
thing that a reader may touch.

Black poets today are becoming increasingly aware of
themselves and their blackness, as they would say, and are
interested in speaking to black people. . . . And I think this
is very important.

In my own poetry I have not abandoned beauty, or
lyricism, and I certainly don't consider myself a "polemical"
poet. I'm just a black poet, and I write about what I see, what
interests me, and I'm seeing new things.

I want to write poems that will be noncompromising. I
don't want to stop a concern with words doing good jobs,
which has always been a concern of mine, but I want to write
poems that will be meaningful to black people . . . things
that will touch them.

The black writer has the American experience and he
also has the black experience [from which to write]; so he's
very rich.*

---

* From "An Interview with Gwendolyn Brooks" in Contemporary Liter-
ature

The Life of Lincoln West

Ugliest little boy
that everyone ever saw.
That is what everyone said.

Even to his mother it was apparent—
when the blue-aproned nurse came into the
northeast end of the maternity ward
bearing his squeals and plump bottom
looped up in a scant receiving blanket,
bending, to pass the bundle carefully
into the waiting mother-hands—that this
was no cute little ugliness, no sly baby waywardness
that was going to inch away
as would baby fat, baby curl, and
baby spot-rash. The pendulous lip, the
branching ears, the eyes so wide and wild,
the vague unvibrant brown of the skin,
and, most disturbing, the great head.
These components of That Look bespoke
the sure fibre. The deep grain.

His father could not bear the sight of him.
His mother high-piled her pretty dyed hair and
put him among her hairpins and sweethearts,
dance slippers, torn paper roses.
He was not less than these,
he was not more.

As the little Lincoln grew,
uglily upward and out, he began
to understand that something was

wrong. His little ways of trying
to please his father, the bringing
of matches, the jumping aside at
warning sound of oh-so-large and
rushing stride, the smile, that gave
and gave and gave—Unsuccessful!

Even Christmases and Easters were spoiled.
He would be sitting at the
family feasting table, really
delighting in the displays of mashed potatoes
and the rich golden
fat-crust of the ham or the festive
fowl, when he would look up and find
somebody feeling indignant about him.

What a pity what a pity. No love
for one so loving. The little Lincoln
loved Everybody. Ants. The changing
caterpillar. His much-missing mother.
His kindergarten teacher.

His kindergarten teacher—whose
concern for him was composed of one
part sympathy and two parts repulsion.
The others ran up with their little drawings.
He ran up with his.
She
tried to be as pleasant with him as
with others, but it was difficult.
For she was all pretty! all daintiness,
all tiny vanilla, with blue eyes and fluffy
sun-hair. One afternoon she
saw him in the hall looking bleak against
the wall. It was strange because the

bell had long since rung and no other
child was in sight. Pity flooded her.
She buttoned her gloves and suggested
cheerfully that she walk him home. She
started out bravely, holding him by the
hand. But she had not walked far before
she regretted it. The little monkey.
Must everyone look? And clutching her
hand like that . . . Literally pinching
it . . .

At seven, the little Lincoln loved
the brother and sister who
moved next door. Handsome. Well-
dressed. Charitable, often, to him. They
enjoyed him because he was
resourceful, made up
games, told stories. But when
their More Acceptable friends came they turned
their handsome backs on him. He
hated himself for his feeling
of well-being when with them despite—
Everything.

He spent much time looking at himself
in mirrors. What could be done?
But there was no
shrinking his head. There was no
binding his ears.

"Don't touch me!" cried the little
fairy-like being in the playground.

Her name was Nerissa. The many
children were playing tag, but when
he caught her, she recoiled, jerked free

and ran. It was like all the
rainbow that ever was, going off
forever, all, all the sparklings in
the sunset west.

One day, while he was yet seven,
a thing happened. In the downtown movies
with his mother a white
man in the seat beside him whispered
loudly to a companion, and pointed at
the little Linc.
"THERE! That's the kind I've been wanting
to show you! One of the best
examples of the species. Not like
those diluted Negroes you see so much of on
the streets these days, but the
real thing.

Black, ugly, and odd. You
can see the savagery. The blunt
blankness. That is the real
thing."

His mother—her hair had never looked so
red around the dark brown
velvet of her face—jumped up,
shrieked "Go to—" She did not finish.
She yanked to his feet the little
Lincoln, who was sitting there
staring in fascination at his assessor. At the author of his
new idea.

All the way home he was happy. Of course,
he had not liked the word
"ugly."
But, after all, should he not

be used to that by now? What had
struck him, among words and meanings
he could little understand, was the phrase
"the real thing."
He didn't know quite why,
but he liked that.
He liked that very much.

When he was hurt, too much
stared at—
too much
left alone—he
thought about that. He told himself
"After all, I'm
the real thing."

It comforted him.

Estimable Mable

"I always think that when I see you you
will like me less than you expected to."

STERLING A. BROWN
[1901–]

worked on the Federal Writer's Project and the Carnegie-Myrdal Study of the Negro. Since 1929 he has been a professor of English at Howard University. His published books include *Southern Road* (1932), *The Negro in American Fiction* (1938), *Negro Poetry and Drama* (1938); and with Arthur P. Davis and Ulysses Lee he edited the classic *Negro Caravan* (1941).

*T*he reading world seems to be ready for a true interpretation of Negro life from within, and poets with a dramatic ability have before them an important task. The world has always been ready for a poet who in his own manner reveals his deepest thoughts and feelings. What it means to be a Negro in the modern world is a revelation much needed in poetry. But the Negro poet must write so that whosoever touches his book touches a man.*

* *From* Negro Poetry and Drama *by Sterling A. Brown*

Slim in Hell

I

Slim Greer went to heaven;
   St. Peter said, "Slim,
You been a right good boy."
   An' he winked at him.

      "You been a travelin' rascal
         In yo' day.
      You kin roam once mo';
         Den you comes to stay.

"Put dese wings on yo' shoulders,
   An' save yo' feet."
Slim grin, and he speak up,
   "Thankye, Pete."

      Den Peter say, "Go
         To Hell an' see,
      All dat is doing, and
         Report to me.

"Be sure to remember
   How everything go."
Slim say, "I be seein' yuh
   On de late watch, bo."

      Slim got to cavortin'
         Swell as you choose,
      Like Lindy in de Spirit
         Of St. Louis Blues.

He flew an' he flew,
   Till at last he hit
A hangar wid de sign readin'
   DIS IS IT.

Den he parked his wings,
An' strolled aroun',
Gittin' used to his feet
On de solid ground.

II

Big bloodhound came aroarin'
Like Niagry Falls,
Sicked on by white devils
In overhalls.

Now Slim warn't scared,
Cross my heart, it's a fac',
An de dog went on a bayin'
Some po' devil's track.

Den Slim saw a mansion
An' walked right in;
De Devil looked up
Wid a sickly grin.

"Suttinly didn't look
Fo' you, Mr. Greer,
How it happen you comes
To visit here?"

Slim say—"Oh, jes' thought
I'd drop by a spell."
"Feel at home, seh, an' here's
De keys to hell."

Den he took Slim around
An' showed him people
Rasin' hell as high as
De First Church Steeple.

Lots of folks fightin'
    At de roulette wheel,
Like old Rampart Street,
    Or leastwise Beale.

Showed him bawdy houses
    An' cabarets,
Slim thought of New Orleans
    An' Memphis days.

Each devil was busy
    Wid a devilish broad,
An' Slim cried, "Lawdy,
    Lawd, Lawd, Lawd."

Took him in a room
    Where Slim see
De preacher wid a brownskin
    On each knee.

Showed him giant stills,
    Going everywhere,
Wid a passel of devils
    Stretched dead drunk there.

Den he took him to de furnace
    Dat some devils was firing,
Hot as hell, an' Slim start
    A mean presspirin'.

White devils wid pitchforks
    Threw black devils on,
Slim thought he'd better
    Be gittin' along.

An' he say—"Dis makes
    Me think of home—

Vicksburg, Little Rock, Jackson,
Waco, and Rome."

Den de devil gave Slim
De big Ha-Ha;
An' turned into a cracker,
Wid a sheriff's star.

Slim ran fo' his wings,
Lit out from de groun'
Hauled it back to St. Peter,
Safety boun'.

III

St. Peter said, "Well,
You got back quick.
How's de devil? An' what's
His latest trick?"

An' Slim say, "Peter,
I really cain't tell,
The place was Dixie
That I took for hell."

Then Peter say, "You must
Be crazy, I vow,
Where'n hell dja think Hell *was,*
Anyhow?

"Git on back to de yearth,
Cause I got de fear,
You'se a leetle too dumb,
Fo' to stay up here . . ."

Southern Road

Swing dat hammer—hunh—
Steady, bo';
Swing dat hammer—hunh—
Steady, bo';
Ain't no rush, bebby,
Long ways to go.

Burner tore his—hunh—
Black heart away;
Burner tore his—hunh—
Black heart away;
Got me life, bebby,
An' a day.

Gal's on Fifth Street—hunh—
Son done gone;
Gal's on Fifth Street—hunh—
Son done gone;
Wife's in de ward, bebby,
Babe's not bo'n.

My ole man died—hunh—
Cussin' me;
My ole man died—hunh—
Cussin' me;
Ole lady rocks, bebby,
Huh misery.

Doubleshackled—hunh—
Guard behin';
Doubleshackled—hunh—
Guard behin';

Ball and chain, bebby,
On my min'.

White man tells me—hunh—
Damn yo' soul;
White man tells me—hunh—
Damn yo' soul;
Got no need, bebby,
To be tole.

Chain gang nevah—hunh—
Let me go;
Chain gang nevah—hunh—
Let me go;
Po' los' boy, bebby,
Evahmo' . . .

Old Lem

I talked to old Lem
And old Lem said:
   "They weigh the cotton
   They store the corn
       We only good enough
       To work the rows;
   They run the commissary
   They keep the books
       We gotta be grateful
       For being cheated;
   Whippersnapper clerks
   Call us out of our name
       We got to say mister
       To spindling boys
   They make our figgers
   Turn somersets
       We buck in the middle
       Say, 'Thankyuh, sah.'
         They don't come by ones
         They don't come by twos
         But they come by tens.

   "They got the judges
   They got the lawyers
   They got the jury-rolls
   They got the law
       They don't come by ones
   They got the sheriffs
   They got the deputies
       They don't come by twos

They got the shotguns
They got the rope
　　We git the justice
　　In the end
　　　　And they come by tens.

"Their fists stay closed
Their eyes look straight
　　Our hands stay open
　　Our eyes must fall
　　　　They don't come by ones
They got the manhood
They got the courage
　　　　They don't come by twos
　　We got to slink around,
　　Hangtailed hounds.
They burn us when we dogs
They burn us when we men
　　　　They come by tens. . . .

"I had a buddy
Six foot of man
Muscled up perfect
Game to the heart
　　　　They don't come by ones
Outworked and outfought
Any man or two men
　　　　They don't come by twos
He spoke out of turn
At the commissary
They gave him a day
To git out the county.
He didn't take it.
He said 'Come and get me.'

They came and got him.
>*And they came by tens.*
He stayed in the county—
He lays there dead.

>*They don't come by ones*
>*They don't come by twos*
>*But they come by tens."*

Strong Men

> *The strong men keep coming on.*
> —Sandburg

They dragged you from homeland,
They chained you in coffles,
They huddled you spoon-fashion in filthy hatches,
They sold you to give a few gentlemen ease.

They broke you in like oxen,
They scourged you,
They branded you,
They made your women breeders,
They swelled your numbers with bastards. . . .
They taught you the religion they disgraced.

You sang:
    Keep a-inchin' along
    Lak a po' inch worm. . . .

You sang:
    Bye and bye
    I'm gonna lay down dis heaby load. . . .

You sang:
    Walk togedder, chillen,
    Dontcha git weary. . . .

      The strong men keep a-comin' on
      The strong men git stronger.

They point with pride to the roads you built for them,
They ride in comfort over the rails you laid for them.
They put hammers in your hands
And said—Drive so much before sundown.

You sang:
>   Ain't no hammah
>   In dis lan',
>   Strikes lak mine, bebby,
>   Strikes lak mine.

They cooped you in their kitchens,
They penned you in their factories,
They gave you the jobs that they were too good for,
They tried to guarantee happiness to themselves
By shunting dirt and misery to you.

You sang:
>   Me an' muh baby gonna shine, shine
>   Me an' muh baby gonna shine.

>>   The strong men keep a-comin' on
>>   The strong men git stronger. . . .

They bought off some of your leaders
You stumbled, as blind men will . . .
They coaxed you, unwontedly soft-voiced. . . .
You followed a way.
Then laughed as usual.
They heard the laugh and wondered;
Uncomfortable;
Unadmitting a deeper terror. . . .

>>   The strong men keep a-comin' on
>>   Gittin' stronger. . . .

What, from the slums
Where they have hemmed you,
What, from the tiny huts
They could not keep from you—
What reaches them
Making them ill at ease, fearful?

Today they shout prohibition at you
"Thou shalt not this"
"Thou shalt not that"
"Reserved for whites only"
You laugh.

One thing they cannot prohibit—

> The strong men . . . coming on
> The strong men gittin' stronger.
> Strong men. . . .
> Stronger. . . .

MARGARET BURROUGHS
[1917–]

received the B.A. and the M.A. degrees in Art Education from the Art Institute of Chicago. Presently, she is director of the DuSable Museum of African-American History, Chicago, and a professor of humanities at Kennedy–King Community College. She is author of *Jasper the Drummin Boy, Did You Feed My Cow? Whip Me Whop Me Pudding,* and *What Shall I Tell My Children Who Are Black?*

I am honored to be included as a "literary godparent of today's black poets" or a "forerunner" so to speak. This properly acknowledges the continuity of our people in the struggle against oppression, from the time when the slavers laid hands on the first Africans down through the centuries to today's liberation fighters. Black poets, from Phillis Wheatley to Margaret Walker and beyond, have played their significant roles by using their pens as their weapons. This is as it should be, has been. Look to the poets. The poets are in the vanguard. If you would stay, thwart progressive change, silence the poets, for if left to their own devices they will prepare the ground for and help to usher in the new order. Jack Conroy said in 1929: "Poets at their best are also prophets, ambassadors of the future, destroyers of the present. They impregnate time with their dreams, and what they conceive, the future delivers. They feel and express what the age lacks. Poets are rebels. The vital rebellion today is centered in the rise of the proletariat. Poets are the pioneers of consciousness. Poets are the affirmers of new values."

I associate myself with these concepts and feel that this is the direction that black poets must take, allied with their white and other singing confrères of the working class if "America is ever to be America again, the land it has never been yet."

Everybody But Me

"You say that you believe in Democracy for everybody, Yes, I know, for dogs and cats and others and everybody, Everybody, but me.

In high sounding words and musty oratory, on Washington's and Lincoln's birthday.

You government officials, major and minor, effuse bright praise to our country and all of her glory.

How it was founded and will always be a haven of the free and I sitting up there listening to you applauded and cheered with all the rest.

But I was one mighty surprised soul to see when it came to the test that you did mean everybody, Everybody, but me.

Sure, I read all about it in the history books about how the founding fathers got together and wrote the Declaration of Independence cause they didn't want King George stepping on them and even though I play a part in bringing it about—they left me out.

They declared that Independence for everybody, Everybody, but me.

They also got together and wrote a Constitution and a Bill of Rights saying that everybody had certain rights and privileges being citizens and that everybody ought to have a job and a place to live and equal opportunity.

But when I tried to get my rights and privileges and a job and a house, I was mighty sorry to find that they really did mean everybody, Everybody, but me.

I went to church every Sunday being a pious person and I heard the preacher talking about heaven and eating milk and honey and wearing long white robes and I felt the spirit and shouted out, shouted out that I wanted to be in the number too.

Suddenly I looked up at the wall, saw that all the folks gathered around Jesus had straw blond hair and sky blue eyes and there wasn't a brother among them, I knew again that they did mean everybody, Everybody, but me.

Of course as far back as I hear tell about there have been times when they needed helping out, this is when they had a war and then they sent out a call for everybody, they knew what to use me for and I found that they really did mean everybody, including me.

My father told me that in World War I they sent out a call for everyone including me and we had to go over to fight the Kaiser to keep the world free and safe for Democracy for everybody.

When I got home I was hurt to find that they really did mean everybody, Everybody, but me.

Well putting two and two together you and I can plainly see that those folks down in Washington have never been thinking of you and me, from here on I'm going to be thinking about me. I'm going to get together with you and my sisters and brothers black and white all over the country and over the world and we're going to put up a terrific fight until we win and we will and when we say peace and freedom for everybody it will mean Everybody, everywhere.

It will mean me."

MARGARET DANNER
[1915–]

has been writing poetry for more than thirty-five years. In 1952 *Poetry* magazine published a series of her poems, "Far From Africa." In 1956 she became assistant editor of the magazine. She has appeared in many anthologies, including *Beyond the Blues*. She has won many awards, and was a recipient of a John Hay Whitney Fellowship.

I have lived long enough to see black poets applying a degree of honesty that augurs well for the salvation of the individuality of one's artistic endeavor. The list is too long to be written here, but their work is proof that the same aesthetic excellence that created the Benin Bronze and the Pyramids is still active today. This patterns my lace and stashes my rainbow.

As for my poetry: I believe that my dharma is to prove that the Force for Good takes precedence over the force for evil in mankind. To the extent that my poetry adheres to this purpose it will endure.

The Rhetoric of Langston Hughes

While some "rap" over this turmoil
of who was Blackest first
and the ins and outs of the Spirituals
and the Blues
and how many of us have or have not
paid our dues;

Langston Hughes (in his traveling)
has sung to so many for so long
and from so very Black a Power
that we have clearly seen the "angles"
and dedicated ourselves
to the unraveling.

At Home in Dakar

When the African Arts,
home again,
became hosts of the hour,
their essence breezed into holidays,
holidays for those
dressed in their tans, browns, and charcoal grays, of the
    West;

and for those robed in their brighter power apparel;
and even for those who had much less than the
seven bright yards of M'bou bous
with the (seemingly) seven bright yards of turban to
    match.
For a flash, their battered sandals and tattered sacs had
    not mattered.

The Art objects (rejoicing in being "at home")
kept lending themselves
until their valid guests were jeweled.

Not one felt too poor
and what with the incessant drumming
we all went on Tribute-to-African-Art inclinations,
Fabio, Fuller, Drake, and Langston Hughes
dancing through the streets.
Yes, I danced, too;
emotions thrumming that the dazzling grace of Blacks
could finally be felt in all its impact

Yes, I danced, too; flinging out
my sheer lace (peach shifting to tangerine) M'bou bou
feeling neither too ill nor too old.

A Grandson is a Hoticeberg

A grandson is
not
the wing-sprouting cherub
that I, as a doting grandmother
have persisted in seeing and showing.

A grandson is a
        hot
            ice
                berg,
that one cannot retain or disdain,
with all the half submerged knowing grinnings,
lusty leerings and/or jeerings
that the name implies.

And as an added distraction or attraction
(according to ones politics)
this grandson is a
            BLACK
                hot
                    ice
                      berg,
with bushy head hung down
and lengthy legs sprawled up
over the easiest-to-dirty chair.

And stubby fingernails thrown out in
"V for victory"
and grubby fists thrust to the polluted air
in cries of
"POWER TO THE PEOPLE . . . FIGHT"

and King Kong combs rearing up out of his
"this is an AFRO . . . MAN" hair.
And orangegreengoldblue
SHIKIS
and ebony with ivory eyed
TIKIS
and rather than the
"Yes mam, grandmother"
that he had been taught;
a jolting of "aints . . . wonts"
and other igniting Black language revolts,
and defyings of
               "RIGHT ON
                         MOTHERS
                                   MOTHER,
          DYNAMITE . . ."

FRANK MARSHALL DAVIS
[1905–]

helped found the great black newspaper *Atlanta Daily World*. His poetry won him a Rosenwald Fellowship, and he is the author of several books of poems: *Black Man's Verse, I Am the American Negro, 47th Street,* and *Through Sepia Eyes.*

I *was black years before I became a poet. I am a social realist. It is the duty of a realistic writer to hold a looking glass to society, mirroring the world he knows while at the same time seeking remedies for glaring ills. And the black poet has, in addition, the special function of helping build black pride as well as baring the falsities surrounding so much of our lives.*

But I see no reason to write our poetry exclusively for a black audience. Although we are victims of racism and white supremacy, these are but loyal and trusted servants of a diseased social order. I cannot foresee the elimination of color prejudice without a radical revision of our entire economic system. For that reason, I write also for white America as in my "To Those Who Sing 'America'" and "Onward Christian Soldiers." I also write about nonracial subjects.

There is a need for the black poet to picture, in the most vividly memorable manner, the black experience. Style and technique are vitally important tools, along with content, if a poem is to have lasting value and not be merely transitory propaganda. Many young black poets have lost sight of these fundamentals and too often substitute annotated graffiti for creativity. There should be rhythmic flow, along with fresh images and phrases, if a poem is to have lasting value. Nevertheless, more are writing today than ever before and no matter how weak and wan the muse, that is a long step forward.

To Those Who Sing America

Well, gentlemen,
You flag wavers
You rabble rousers
You who ask that I sing America
On patriotic occasions—
Here is one question:
What do you know of the song you chant?
You begin
"My country! 'tis of thee"
But here the patter ends.
Gentlemen,
Haven't you forgotten
Something?

● ● ●

"My country! 'tis of thee, . . ."
(*On the shores of this, my country, dwell Plenty in a
forty-room mansion and Poverty in a one-room hovel
. . . cotton growers starving, wheat raisers naked
. . . a nation turned prostitute for the fat pimps of
Politicians and Captains of Industry . . . Sundays
all rise to serve a crippled Nordic God . . . His
torn-out eyes replaced by dollar signs . . . His belly
bloated with the greasy gravy of the Profit System
. . . His spindly paralyzed shanks moulded from the
spavined bones of the hungry workers . . . his dod-
dering frame supported by the props of Federal
Dole and Government Subsidy . . . this is my coun-
try with the star spangled robe snatched away*)
"Sweet land of liberty, . . ."
(*Do you remember Sacco and Vanzetti in Boston, Tom
Mooney in California, nine Scottsboro boys in Ala-
bama?*)

"Of thee I sing; . . ."
(*Yes—with words approved by the (no longer important)*
Granddaughters of the American Revolution, Ku
Klux Klan, American Legion, Federal Council of
Churches and Boards of Censors of forty-eight
states)
"Land where my fathers died! . . ."
(*While strong-arming the Indian owners . . . starving to*
fill money sacks of Mistermorgan, Misterdupont,
Mistermellon . . . human guinea pigs testing crazy
social systems)
"Land of the Pilgrims' pride! . . ."
(*The pilgrims, gentlemen, had not seen my country as a*
land of peons down South, wage-slaves up North
. . . her wooded hills stripped to stony nakedness
by lumber corporations . . . signboards selling beer
and bunion cures blocking her native scenery . . .
lynched black bodies swaying from trees in a morn-
ing breeze)
"From ev'ry mountain side . . ."
(*Including airy skyscraper and penthouse for the few,*
disease-cradling tenement for the many)
"Let freedom ring!"
(*Although the rich are counting dividends and dodging*
income taxes while the poor are scrambling for
crumbs dropped from the Table of Capitalism, let
us hush . . . the Politicians and Professional Ameri-
cans would lift their voices in song)

●   ●   ●

We shall stop here
My flag waving friends
You don't remember
The other verses
Anyway. . . .

Dancing Gal

Black and tan—yeah, black and tan
Spewing the moans of a jigtime band
What does your belly crave?
    A brown-sugar brown
    Slim gal sways
    Pretzel twisting
    Beneath a yellow thumb
    Of steel-stiff light
    Amid a striped rain
    Of red-note, blue-note

    Jazz-hot jazz
    Gazelle graceful
    Lovely as a lover's dream
    Silken skinned, stillwater soft
    Young girl breasts in gold encased
    Scant gold around her lower waist
    Red lips parted
    Dark eyes flashing
    She dances
    Dips, whirls, undulates
    Her body a living chord
    Set loud and sweet
    Against the bitter quiet
    Of drab and muted human shapes

    I see a long lean god
    Standing in painted splendor

"Onward Christian Soldiers!"

The religion of Sweet Jesus
The spirit of Our Saviour
March on
With missionaries
And civilization
Into darkest Africa

Day by day
Black folk learn
Rather than with
A heathen spear
'Tis holier to die
By a Christian gun . . .

OWEN DODSON
[1914–]

was for many years chairman of the Drama Department of Howard University. He has also been artistic consultant at the Harlem School of the Arts. His poetry has been included in over thirty-five anthologies, and he has written two volumes entitled *Powerful Long Ladder* and *The Confession Stone*. Dodson is also the author of a novel, *Boy at the Window*. He has been the recipient of the Maxwell Anderson Verse Award, a Guggenheim Fellowship, and a Rockefeller Fellowship.

I think my poetry is modest in contrast to the plain, broken bread and broken-toothed irony of our poets. So many of them have written with force, the brightness of youth, in a noise of what the ceilings of our hopes should be, and must be.

Between the age of Langston Hughes and Countee Cullen and my age, I think there must be a deep-felt relationship with our times and our hopes. Somehow or other, in your new generation, the rush is so fast—the pace has nooks and crannies and pitch balls that trap so many of our new, younger writers. But after this interim generation, "I CALL ME BLACK," there is a new one emerging that is conscious of craftsmanship and hope hanging on our blooming trees.

How can our young writers behold their new world without the old world, and the sharp horizon where the sun will create an enormous life of credibility in the darkness where most of the world dwells?

The Morning Duke Ellington Praised the Lord and Six Little Black Davids Tapped Danced Unto

The morning Duke Ellington praised the Lord
The stars plus the moon shone out loud—
Six little black Davids
Tapped danced unto:
Gabriel trumpeted up arthritic Michael:
Plus some Archangels who had slipped from grace
Into Hell when God rode like a roaring
General of peace into the universe.
Trumpets: who whee, who wheee——
Duke's horns, all his brasses plus drums
Did a dip pip pip-a-de doo.
Duke now called out: "Recite the books!"
Trumpets, and all brasses plus thumping piano,
Plus triumphant chorus—
Sang, wailed, beat, spit out
Under the cymbals and the drums and the brass plates:
Of Bible sin and redemption:

Now! who whooee—a dip-a-de do: now, come on:
Genesis, Exodus, Leviticus:
Now Chorus: "In the beginning God created
The Heavens and the earth."
Whooee, wee, whooeee, whoohee
Joy amazing glory in the books of God:
Ruth, Naomi, Daniel plus Hosiah and Malachi

And so forth and what not; my testimony
Is with Judges:
"Don't judge me!
"Yes, judge me—yes put me, me on the witness stand."
Let the trumpets blow the candles out
Then Naomi can kiss the cross in the dark.
Do a dip-a-de do.
Ruth lights them again
To make the wailing wall of darkness
A pillar of light, Whoee, ooee, whoee
Duke's drums are cymbals
The trumpets spit back a dance:
Then there is doomsday and eternity
Sitting on your black entrails.
Duke knows the stained-glassed window
Of Christ will fall down.
Does he want it on his back?
He doesn't want anything
But Genesis, Numbers, Malachi, Leviticus, and so forth
Where is God with his watermelon, and dandelion wine?
Mary Magdalene has a fit when she sees
Jesus when, she is eighty-eight—
Whoo-whee-whee—her eyes are glazed
As Jesus presents her manna
Milk and honey, but no dandelion wine.
He bends over as a father:
He was thirty-three when he ended.
Naomi has a do amid the alien corn—
While Ruth devours wheat.
Duke's drums and cymbals and trumpets:
Holler whoo-whoo-whee.
Deuteronomy, Zakariah, Luke,
John the Divine who loved Jesus
Corinthians: "When I was a man I spoke as a man."

Up the altar
Six Black Davids
Tapped danced praise unto.
Jesus becomes cloud—whooee—whoo-ee—whooee—
No one is here but Duke and his black boys.
We hear the trumpet of Gabriel through it all.
He has called the children home.
Is that your combo, Duke?
Right on!
Six black boys still tap dance up the marble altar praising
    unto.
Hallelujah to tomorrow.
A dip-a-do,
A dip-a-dip
A dip-a-de-do. Do!

Ballad of Badmen

There's a band of men who roam this land:
No one knows how many
They have no leader
They don't know each other;
Each are marked like Cain
Their scars show only in the brain, my God
Their scars show only in the brain.

They plucked brother Abel's freckles for supper
To toss them into the tasty stew:
They howl if the freckles are few, my God,
They howl if the freckles are few.

I saw them kick his old mother downstairs:
They laughed that old mother in fun and joy
As she died at the foot of the stairs, my God
In an agony of blood she was kicked into death.
They ate her freckles too, my God,
They gobbled her freckles too.

They shrieked and returned to brother Abel again
(in the barbarous forests where love is dead)
To rip him naked and rape him there
In their ratty lair, one by one they raped him there, my
    God:
In their ratty lair they stripped off his skin
And they tore at the flesh,
They cracked on his bones,
Made signs of the cross
And knelt pious knees to you and to me, my God.
They prayed in the slime of the night
For more my God, for more my God, for more
My God, my God, my God for more.

Job's Ancient Lament

God, why have you ruined me,
What have I done unto thee
Except to worship the seasons
Of your health and the fruit
Of your blood in the earth.
I have prospered for you
I have prayed by your waters,
Slept in the rushes, handled a star,
Been burned to my vitals:
All as you commanded.
Where have I faltered?
Where have I failed?
Why have you ruined me?

God, isn't mercy Your purpose?
Are these boils the growth of Your Grace?
Have my boys died because I created
Wings for them to fly (ICARUS one and two)
To pray in thy kingdom
Before our dead day of your dry doom?
Are they lost near the sun?
Thousands of voices
Mourn for them
Sea anemones turn black to
Mourn for them,
Processions of sisters, mothers, brothers, and syphilitic
    sons
Walk the waters to repent,
Bleed themselves to
Mourn for them toward

Their day of doom.
When two locked trunks
Tumbled from the sky into my garden:
I opened them: and there:
Trussed up inside like table turkeys: were my boys:
My wife went blind, my boils burst
Blackbirds and larks sang no more,
Daisies lost their golden eyes,
Children refused to play
Flames from mortal temples
Burnt out the countryside: the world!
Will they reach the sky?
God, why have you ruined us?

ROBERT HAYDEN
[1913–]

is currently professor of English at the University of
Michigan. His poetry won the Grand Prize for Poetry
at the First World Festival of Negro Art at Dakar,
Senegal. His published works include *Heart-Shape in
the Dusk*, *A Ballad of Remembrance*, *Selected Poems*,
and *Words in the Mourning Time*.

*B*eing *a poet is role enough, and special enough. What else can I say? I object to strict definitions of what a poet is or should be, because they usually are thought up by people with an axe to grind—by those who care less about poetry than they do about some cause. We're living in a time when individuality is threatened by a kind of mechanizing anonymity. And by regimentation. In order to be free, you must submit to tyranny, to ideological slavery, in the name of freedom. And, obviously, this is the enemy of the artist; it stultifies anything creative. Which brings me to my own view of the role of the poet, the artist. I am convinced that if poets have any calling, function,* raison d'être *beyond the attempt to produce viable poems—and that in itself is more than enough—it is to affirm the humane, the universal, the potentially divine in the human creature. And I'm sure the artist does this best by being true to his or her own vision and to the demands of the art. This is my view; it's the conviction out of which I write. I do not set it up as an imperative for others.*

Poetry, all art, it seems to me, is ultimately religious in the broadest sense of the term. It grows out of, reflects, illuminates our inmost selves, and so on. It doesn't have to be sectarian or denominational. There's a tendency today—more than a tendency, it's almost a conspiracy—to delimit poets, to restrict them to the political and the socially or racially conscious. To me, this indicates gross ignorance of the poet's true function as well as of the function and value of poetry as art. With a few notable exceptions, poets have generally been on the side of justice and humanity. I can't imagine any poet worth his salt today not being aware of social evils, human needs. But I feel I have the right to deal with these matters in my own way, in terms of my own understanding of what a poet is. I resist whatever would force me into a role as politician, sociologist, or yea-sayer to current ideologies. I know who I am, and pretty much what I want to say.*

* *From* Interviews with Black Writers, *edited by John O'Brien*

Richard Hunt's Arachne

Human face becoming locked insect face
    mouth of agony shaping a cry it cannot utter
        eyes bulging brimming with the horrors
           of her becoming

        Dazed crazed
    by godly vivisection husking her
gutting her
cutting hubris its fat and bones away

In goggling terror fleeing powerless to flee
    Arachne not yet arachnid and no longer woman
        in the moment's centrifuge of dying
          becoming

The Night-Blooming Cereus

And so for nights
we waited, hoping to see
the heavy bud
    break into flower.

On its neck-like tube
hooking down from the edge
of the leaf-branch
    nearly to the floor,

the bud packed
tight with its miracle swayed
stiffly on breaths
    of air, moved

as though impelled
by stirrings within itself.
It repelled as much
    as it fascinated me

sometimes—snake,
eyeless bird head,
beak that would gape
    with grotesque life-squawk.

But you, my dear,
conceded less to the bizarre
than to the imminence
    of bloom. Yet we agreed

we ought
to celebrate the blossom,

paint ourselves, dance
in honor of

archaic mysteries
when it appeared. Meanwhile
we waited, aware
of rigorous design.

Backster's
polygraph, I thought,
would have shown
(as clearly as it had

a philodendron's
fear) tribal sentience
in the cactus, focused
energy of will.

That belling of
tropic perfume—that
signaling
not meant for us;

the darkness
cloyed with summoning
fragrance. We dropped
trivial tasks

and marveling
beheld at last the achieved
flower. Its moonlight
petals were

still unfold-
ing, the spike fringe of the outer
perianth recessing
as we watched.

Lunar presence,
foredoomed, already dying,
it charged the room
   with plangency

older than human
cries, ancient as prayers
invoking Osiris, Krishna,
   Tezcátlipóca.

We spoke
in whispers when
we spoke
   at all . . .

The Peacock Room

(in memory of Betsy Graves Reyneau)

Ars Longa　　　Which is crueller
Vita Brevis　　　life or art?
　　　Thoughts in the Peacock Room,
where briefly I shelter. As in the glow
(remembered or imagined?)
　　　of the lamp shaped like a rose
my mother would light
for me some nights to keep
　　　Raw-Head-And-Bloody-Bones away.

Exotic, fin de siècle, unreal
and beautiful the Peacock Room.
　　　Triste metaphor.
Hiroshima　　　Watts　　　My Lai.
Thus history scorns
　　　the vision chambered in gold
and Spanish leather, lyric space;
rebukes, yet cannot give the lie
　　　to what is havened here.

Environment as ornament.
Whistler with arrogant art designed
　　　it, mocking a connoisseur
with satiric arabesque of gold
peacocks on a wall peacock blue
　　　in fury trampling coins of gold.
Such vengeful harmonies drove
a rival mad. As in a dream
　　　I see the crazed young man.

He shudders in a corner, shields

his face in terror of
        the perfect malice of those claws.
She too is here—ghost
of the happy child she was that day.
        When I turned twelve,
they gave me for a birthday gift
a party in the Peacock Room.
        With shadow cries

the peacocks flutter down,
their spread tails concealing her,
        then folding, drooping to reveal
her eyeless, old–Med School
cadaver, flesh-object
        pickled in formaldehyde,
who was artist, compassionate,
clear-eyed. Who was belovéd friend.
        No more. No more.

The birds resume their splendored pose.
And Whistler's portrait of
        a tycoon's daughter gleams
like imagined flowers. What is art?
What is life?
        What the Peacock Room?
Rose-leaves and ashes drift
its portals, gently spinning towards
        a bronze bodhisattva's ancient smile.

LANCE JEFFERS
[1919–]

holds an honors degree from Columbia University. His work has appeared in *The Best American Short Stories* and *Dasein*. His second volume of poetry, *When I Know the Power of My Black Hand*, will soon be published by Broadside Press.

I believe that the future of black poetry lies on two foundationstones: (1) continued rage and protest, continued vehement criticism of oppression and the oppressor and American society, and (2) careful analysis of blackfolk.

Black literature is based to a very considerable extent on the first foundation, and this foundation will exist so long as the white man continues to define a subordinate role for the black man in American society, so long as the white man continues to define a subordinate role for any other people on this planet. In other words, until American society as we know it is utterly demolished, exploded into dust, angry protest will continue. And must continue.

But the second foundation has yet really to emerge: the systematic exploration of the infinite complexity of the black personality in America. We are only beginning to discover who we are, and I suspect that we frequently flinch before the knowledge of ourselves. We have, like the rest of humanity, numerous masks behind which we hide. And many of the masks are fashionable and attractive.

Who are we?

There have been writers in the past, in the relatively distant past and in the recent past (James Weldon Johnson, Wright, Ellison, Baraka), who have asked this question. I believe that the uterus of inexorable change, the uterus of history, will birth a procession of writers who will tear the masks from our faces and reveal us to ourselves in a poetry that will combine history and protest and demand and rage and relentless self-probing, a proud womanly and manly seekforth exploration of the unexplored continents of black nature in America: the womb of ultimate grandeur in black poetry.

We will be the masters of our destiny—and our poetry will help to sweep the way.

Black Soul of the Land

I saw an old black man walk down the road,
a Georgia country road.
I stopped and asked where the nearest town might lie
where I could find a meal.
I might have driven on then to the town nearby
but I stayed to talk to the old black man
and read the future in his eyes.

His face was leathered, lean and strong,
gashed with struggle scars.
His eyes were piercing, weary, red,
but in the old grief-soul that stared
through his eyes at me
and in the humble frame bent with humiliation and age,
there stood a secret manhood tough and tall
that circumstance and crackers could not kill:
a secret spine unbent within a spine,
a secret source of steel,
a secret sturdy rugged love,
a secret crouching hate,
a secret knife within his hand,
a secret bullet in his eye.

Give me your spine, old man, old man,
give me your rugged hate,
give me your sturdy oak-tree love,
give me your source of steel.
Teach me to sing so that the song may be mine
"Keep your hands on the plow: hold on!"
One day the nation's soul shall turn black like yours
and America shall cease to be its name.

Trellie

From the old slave shack I chose my lady,
from the harsh garden of the South,
from the South's black children,
from the old slaves bending between the rows of cotton,
from Charlie James whose soul was African in
　　the unredeeming Southern sun,
from the song of slaves who choked the sky like
　　chitlins down their throats,
from the woman dark who stood and leaned back as
　　Southern women do, her stomach out, her shoulders
　　　back,
　　and wombed the grandeur of her poetry in song as
　　long and deep as prehistoric night,
in song as causeful as the fiery center of the earth,
in love as muscular as the thighs of
　　darkskinned god who cradled Africa to his chest,
in love as nippled as the milk that flows from Nile to sea:

She lies beside me in the night
　　who is the greatness of the slaves without their fear,
she is the anger of this day and elegant pride
　　that touched the child who walked three miles to
　　school and saw white children's bus leave her trampling
　　in the dust:

There is a beauty here that I aspire:
there is a grandeur here that I require:
the Southern loam to throw into the sandbags of my soul,
some other rapture that my song must lyre,
some woollier head to batter the entombment of my fire,
to lay my stunted heart upon the pyre and blow upon

my godliness till it come down my mouth,
the soul of my grandfather's sire
when he stood harried in slavery.

As I lie beside her in the night I see America's
    birth in death
and tyranny grind its knife to seek my veins,
I see myself in prison camp alone,
hooking the guillotine's eye to my neckflesh when
        morning come,
and she weeping and engrieved within my breast.

What more marrowed sorrow could there be
when tear as large as blackness' pyramid will lodge my
        eye
    and drop, when my blood prepares to sink beneath the
        soil?
But Trellie's brothers
    will run the reindeer down from frozen North
and bring her love to me within my grave,
and all my whiter crimes and grudging heart,
and all my assassination of myself,
and all my children's New World conquering will grow
        like
    elephant tusks from earth I drenched in blood,
ten thousand children will redwood from my genes
    to mount the earth in my black people's time!

Love Pictures You as Black and Long-faced

Love pictures you as black and long-faced,
sweet to the black-faced lover's eye,
torn, the secret gut of you,
with a cracker's bleeding thigh,
and the sweet-thorned creation's core of you
    bleeds from a child's cry.

Ah woman blacked with Africa's rising dust,
and swamped with the moon-water's rust and
the white man's scythe-armed lust,

in your wheat-strewn bed's the planetary gust
of your people's victory!

OLIVER La GRONE
[1906–]

is a graduate of the University of New Mexico. His works have appeared in many anthologies: *Beyond the Blues, For Malcolm, New Negro Poets, The Poetry of the Negro 1746–1970, New Black Voices, The American Equation,* and *They Speak of Dawns.* He is also one of the country's leading sculptors and lecturers in black history and art.

*D*r. W. E. B. Du Bois in the title "Souls of Black Folk"
brought together "black" and "soul" in 1903, sixty years before
a new generation of black youth rediscovered its significance
in their search for an identity with dignity. Its message was
reinforced in his "Black Reconstruction" so there is more than
a "kernel of truth" in the jingle, "Du Bois in 1903 named it,
black youth in 1963 claimed it."

As new chapters continue to unfold in this odyssey of the
Afro-American and his art as an integral part of his life and
world history, black poets, I think, will celebrate the bitter
trials and defeats, the angry struggles and victories, and hope-
fully the tears and laughter of all those generations of the
voiceless and invisible peoples without loudspeakers or bill-
boards.

As an artist guided only by insights, poetry for me is a
very personal, and yet a group art, expression. I like a latitude
suited to my views about two areas of art in which I work,
sculpture and poetry. Consciously, the social muse tells me
that the black face is yet to be "seen" in America and the
world. So, I am likely to go on pursuing eclecticism in poetry
and sculpture—manipulating materials, ideas, and concepts in
image-making acts that to date have no common signature.
The idea, concept, and form I would keep as elements to be
brought into final harmony as an "entity" freed of schools and
philosophies—the craft and skills a growing tool. I would wish
to remember that bias, ethnicity, and ideology may or may not
be the enemy of art, but that craft and skill are color blind.

Remnant Ghosts at Dawn

Vultures waft circles
In lazy Afric skies
Graced wings glide down
The hungry eyes
Vigilings . . .

The deflate lizard swells
And quick away
Stops
Head lifts and jerks
In sharp alerts
To right and left
Looking listening . . .
No walk or hall
No trench or wall
Can make it stay
(Not one to be a captive
or at bay.)

In mouth of portugals
Old cannon sunning
The scaly lounger ploys
His never ending play
No sentry's stomp
Or flintlock sound
Now sends him
Scurrying away
A vagrant with a mission . . .

Brass cannon cankered
The reptile lazing

The vulture at scavage
And the gate-guard gone
Ghosts and remnants
Of the bitter chapter
Of other days when the
Slavers' craze was
Lust for the prize
In the black-gold pawn . . .
Where history stands
Frozen for new eyes
At break of another dawn . . .

For Kinte
(*For Alex*)

> *In the beginning was the word.*
> —John 1: 1

You would not bend
Kinte
Your word and act
Were one
(Broke link and chain)
Two centuries of seed
Would feed upon
As earth-poured springs—
As roots that would not die
In veldt or occan
Strange land and climc
The spirit sings
To resurrect with pride
The tall proud cry . . .
That would not bend . . .

Tale Teller moving
To reclaim the word-lit path
(Where lash and sundered leg
Unbent and upright spine
The stolen name of family line
The yesterday and yesterplace)
Recovered yours and mine
The saga of a pcoplc
Snatched from living limbo
Rejoined to life
In time and space.

Africland

From breasts
Of Africland
I suck the suns
Fan
By the palm frond winds
Of oceaned breathings . . .
Rapt thoughts
My eyes
Quest wanderings
That agonize
Fix the broad brood
And break of
Many-mooded mask
In wave-roll-surge
Hiding tales
Down down
Under fluid vaults
Of darkened time . . .
A light I ask.

(In retrospect of
Ingrown pain
Assuage desired
That seeks this veil
To throw
Relieve the secret cocoon
Chapters locked below
This birthing . . .
These roots of yestertimes)
The shark Teeth raiding

The domain of wake
In middle-passage
Cut the umbilical cord
Coffle
Stolen name
And lash
Set me adrift in
Shackles of ingenuous greed . . .

Now reverie
Before beginnings
Long diasporas till yet
Shrouded in the mist and main
The cry
Circumstance
Through season sea
And sky
Pulled by a shore bound host
That taunt the ear and bid
The eye
Insistent . . .

The fretted ebon limbs
Beat weavings in the
Drum-chant-dance
On earth with ancient
Orgies and rhythmed
Hymns . . .
Taletellers celebrate
The spirit-act
Before the mother womb
Over the roar of
Aged cryptic silences . . .

Necklace cloth
And image in the round

They do not
Bind shackle halt
My hands move underground
For mines of men
My fathers footsteps
Then to now and when

I stride the ocean floors
Of whited bones
Calling across the night
I find dark teats
Of motherland
To drink a new worlds
Breaking light.

NAOMI LONG MADGETT
[1923–]

was first published when she was seventeen years old. Her publications include *One and the Many* (1956), *Star by Star* (1965), and *Pink Ladies in the Afternoon* (1972). Her poems have been included in over fifty anthologies in this country and abroad. Presently, Ms. Madgett is Professor of English at Eastern Michigan University in Ypsilanti and publisher and associate editor of Lotus Press in Detroit.

I *don't see myself as a "forerunner" of anything or anyone. I write today and am so involved in this present that the past and future pretty much take care of themselves.*

In various ways, I have touched the lives of several younger poets whom we are hearing from now, and I have always tried to encourage them and, whenever the occasion has arisen, to teach them, but I am not aware that any of them (except perhaps one) have been visibly influenced. It may be better that way.

The labels I frequently see according to age-groupings seem somewhat meaningless. If I am a "torchbearer" or a "literary godparent," I am not aware of it. Age is an artificial factor, I think, as the five decades of Langston Hughes's productivity and continued relevance bear out.

That I am indebted to him and other poets of the past is obvious. I teethed on their work and, sometimes in very personal ways, some of them encouraged me—Langston and Countee Cullen, in particular. I would be happy to feel that younger poets might say the same of me, but it will take posterity to tell that. I think we are too close to the scene to know what will have any permanence.

I have tried to be as honest and as independent in my work as I know how. Poetry written by blacks is necessarily black poetry. Everything I see and everything I write is sifted through a fine mesh of black consciousness and that consciousness has colored all of my perceptions. I hope my poems are better for that added sensitivity, and I hope that others who come after me will see their experiences mirrored in mine. That is all I can hope for.

Simple

(For Langston Hughes)

He sits at the bar in the Alhambra
looking down Seventh Avenue
through the open door.
He wants to talk, but the stool beside
         him
is empty
and no one he knows is coming down the
         street.

    Hey man, I got problems—ya know?
    Could ya let me have another fin
    jes' till nex' Friday, huh?
    I gotta get in to change my clothes
    but my lan'lady's bolted the door
         again.
    If Joyce don't get to go to that
         show
    again tonight, man,
    my name really be mud!

The landlady's bolted the door for good
this time
and he will never go home.

Joyce will tap her toe impatiently
         awhile
and then go out alone.
through a long, long night

he will stare at his empty beer glass
and the vacant stool
and soon he will wonder what it was
he wanted to say.

Black Woman

My hair is springy like the forest grasses
That cushion the feet of squirrels—
Crinkled and blown in a south breeze
Like the small leaves of native bushes.

My black eyes are coals burning
Like a low, full, jungle moon
Through the darkness of being.
In a clear pool I see my face,
Know my knowing.

My hands move pianissimo
Over the music of the night:
Gentle birds fluttering through leaves and grasses
They have not always loved,
Nesting, finding home.

Where are my lovers?
Where are my tall, my lovely princes
Dancing in slow grace
Toward knowledge of my beauty?
Where
Are my beautiful
Black men?

Woman with Flower

I wouldn't coax the plant if I were you.
Such watchful nurturing may do it harm.
Let the soil rest from so much digging
And wait until it's dry before you water it.
The leaf's inclined to find its own direction;
Give it a chance to seek the sunlight for itself.

Much growth is stunted by too careful prodding,
Too eager tenderness.
The things we love we have to learn to leave alone.

Offspring

I tried to tell her:
    This way the twig is bent.
    Born of my trunk and strengthened by my roots,
    You must stretch newgrown branches
    Closer to the sun
    Than I can reach.
I wanted to say:
    Extend my self to that far atmosphere
    Only my dreams allow.

But the twig broke,
And yesterday I saw her
Walking down an unfamiliar street,
    Feet confident,
    Face slanted upward toward a threatening sky,
    And
    She was smiling
    And she was
    Her very free,
    Her very individual,
    Unpliable
    Own.

DUDLEY RANDALL
[1914–]

is the publisher of Broadside Press in Detroit. Through Broadside Press he has given many black poets the opportunity to have their works published. He is the editor of *The Black Poets, Black Poetry,* and *For Malcolm* (with Margaret Burroughs); and the author of *Poem Counterpoem* (with Margaret Danner), *Cities Burning, Love You, More to Remember,* and *After the Killing.*

*M*y view of poetry today is optimistic. Not only are poets scattered over the whole country, instead of being concentrated in Chicago or New York, but they are constantly moving—teaching and learning in new places. Stephany moved from Chicago to Berkeley to Chicago, Baraka from New York to San Francisco to Newark, Margaret Danner from Chicago to Detroit to Richmond to Memphis, Ishmael Reed from Buffalo to Berkeley. Also, the poets are stretching and growing. In their recent books, Hayden, Baraka, Brooks, and Madhubuti showed change and growth. Because of the emergence of black bookstores and publishers, poets no longer have to depend on Random House or Morrow to be published. The older poets like Hayden, Brooks, Walker, and Sterling Brown are still producing, and act as guides and inspiration for younger poets.

In my own poetry, I no longer strive for the intricate, sonorous stanzas of "The Southern Road." I try for a looser form, a more colloquial diction, as in "Frederick Douglass and the Slave Breaker." I want my poems to be read and understood by children, students, farmers, factory workers, professors. I seek directness and lucidity, but also a richness so that the reader will find added meanings on each new reading. Although these are my goals, it does not necessarily follow that I shall attain them.

Green Apples

What can you do with a woman under thirty?
It's true she has a certain freshness, like a green apple,
but how raw, unformed, without the mellowness of maturity.

What can you talk about with a young woman?
That is, if she gives you a chance to talk,
as she talks and talks and talks about herself.
Her   self   is the most important object in the universe.
She lacks the experience of intimate, sensitive silences.

Why don't young women learn how to make love?
They attack with the subtlety of a bull,
and moan and sigh with the ardor of a puppy.
Panting, they pursue their own pleasure,
forgetting to please their partner, as an older woman does.

It's only just that young women get what they deserve.
A young man.

On Getting a Natural
(For Gwendolyn Brooks)

She didn't know she was beautiful,
though her smiles were dawn,
her voice was bells,
and her skin deep velvet Night.

She didn't know she was beautiful,
although her deeds,
kind, generous, unobtrusive,
gave hope to some,
and help to others,
and inspiration to us all. And
beauty is as beauty does,
they say.

Then one day there blossomed
a crown upon her head,
bushy, bouffant, real Afro-down,
Queen Nefertiti again.
And now her regal wooly crown
declares,
I know
I'm black
AND
beautiful.

Langston Blues

Your lips were so laughing
Langston man
your lips were so singing
minstrel man
how death could touch them
hard to understand

Your lips that laughed
and sang so well
your lips that brought
laughter from hell
are silent now
no more to tell

So let us sing
a Langston blues
sing a lost
Langston blues
long gone song
for Langston Hughes

MARGARET WALKER
[1915–]

is the author of the classic *For My People* and the highly praised novel *Jubilee,* and the coauthor of *A Poetic Equation: Conversations Between Nikki Giovanni and Margaret Walker.* She is currently teaching and residing in Mississippi.

*I*t is a fact that some of the most significant poetry written in America during the past two decades has been written by . . . [blacks]. Now, what is the promise? Is there hope that it will be fulfilled? Is the . . . [black] poet doomed to annihilation because he is part of a doomed Western world, or is that Western culture really doomed? Is our society already a fascist society? If it is, what hope has our literature? If these are only bogeymen, then whither are we turning? Is our path toward religious revival, neoclassicism, internationalism a result of global perspectives and world government, or what?

The future of the . . . [black poet] in America is bright only if the future of the world is bright, and if he with the rest of his world can survive the deadly conflicts that threaten him and his total freedom, the awful anticipation of which now hangs over his head like the sword of Damocles.*

* *From* Phylon *Magazine*

Ballad of the Hoppy-Toad

Ain't been on Market Street for nothing
With my regular washing load
When the Saturday crowd went stomping
Down the Johnny-jumping road,

Seen Sally Jones come running
With a razor at her throat,
Seen Deacon's daughter lurching
Like a drunken alley goat.

But the biggest for my money,
And the saddest for my throw
Was the night I seen the goopher man
Throw dust around my door.

Come sneaking round my doorway
In a stovepipe hat and coat;
Come sneaking round my doorway
To drop the evil note.

I run down to Sis Avery's
And told her what I seen
"Root-worker's out to git me
What you reckon that there mean?"

Sis Avery she done told me,
"Now honey go on back
I knows just what will hex him
And that old goopher sack."

Now I done burned the candles
Till I seen the face of Jim

And I done been to Church and prayed
But can't git rid of him.

Don't want to burn his picture
Don't want to dig his grave
Just want to have my peace of mind
And make that dog behave.

Was running through the fields one day
Sis Avery's chopping corn
Big horse come stomping after me
I knowed then I was gone.

Sis Avery grabbed that horse's mane
And not one minute late
Cause trembling down behind her
I seen my ugly fate.

She hollered to that horse to "Whoa!
I gotcha hoppy-toad."
And yonder come the goopher man
A-running down the road.

She hollered to that horse to "Whoa"
And what you wanta think?
Great-God-a-mighty, that there horse
Begun to sweat and shrink.

He shrunk up to a teeny horse
He shrunk up to a toad
And yonder come the goopher man
Still running down the road.

She hollered to that horse to "Whoa"
She said, "I'm killing him.
Now you just watch this hoppy-toad
And you'll be rid of Jim."

The goopher man was hollering
"Don't kill that hoppy-toad."
Sis Avery she said "Honey,
You bout to lose your load."

That hoppy-toad was dying
Right there in the road
And goopher man was screaming
"Don't kill that hoppy-toad."

The hoppy-toad shook one more time
And then he up and died
Old goopher man fell dying, too.
"O hoppy-toad," he cried.

Jackson, Mississippi

City of tense and stricken faces
City of closed doors and ketchup splattered floors,
City of barbed wire stockades,
And ranting voices of demagogues,
City of squealers and profane voices;
Hauling my people in garbage trucks,
Fenced in by new white police billies,
Fist cuffs and red-necked brothers of Hate Legions
Straining their leashed and fiercely hungry dogs;
City of tree-lined, wide, white avenues
And black alleys of filthy rendezvous;
City of flowers: of new red zinnias
And oriental poppies and double-ruffled petunias
Ranch styled houses encircled with rose geranium
And scarlet salvia
And trouble-ridden minds of the guilty and the
　　conscienceless;
City of stooges and flunkeys, pimps and prostitutes,
Bar-flies and railroad-station freaks;
City with Southern sun beating down raw fire
On heads of blaring jukes,
And light-drenched streets puddled with the promise
Of a brand-new tomorrow
I give you my heart, Southern City
For you are my blood and dust of my flesh,
You are the harbor of my ship of hope,
The dead-end street of my life,
And the long washed down drain of my youth's years of
　　toil,
In the bosom of your families

I have planted my seeds of dreams and visions and
  prophecies
All my fantasies of freedom and of pride,
Here lie three centuries of my eyes and my brains and
  my hands,
Of my lips and strident demands,
The graves of my dead,
And the birthing stools of grannies long since fled.

Today

I

I sing of slum scabs on city faces, scrawny children scarred by bombs and dying of hunger, wretched human scarecrows strung against lynching stakes, those dying of pellagra and silicosis, rotten houses falling on slowly decaying humanity.

I sing of Man's struggle to be clean, to be useful, to be free; of need arising from our lives, of bitter living flowing in our laughter, of cankerous mutiny eating through the nipples of our breasts.

I sing of our soon-to-be-dead, of last escape: drunkard raising flasks to his lips never tasting the solace, gambler casting his last die never knowing the win, lover seeking lips of the beloved never tasting fruit of his kiss, never knowing the languorous sleep.

I sing these fragments of living that you may know by these presents that which we feared most has come upon us.

II

You walking these common neighboring streets with no disturbing drone of bombing planes, no Sunday air-raiding, and no shells caving in roofs of your houses; fearing no severed baby arms nor naked eyeballs hurtled in your hands; riding trolley and jitney daily, buying gas and light hourly, viewing weekly "Wild West Indian and Shooting Sam," "Mama Loves Papa," and

"Gone by the Breeze," complacently smug in a snug somnolescence;

You in Middle America distantly removed from Middle Europe, no closer than morning headlines and evening news flashes, bothered by petty personals— your calories and eyemaline, your henna rinse and dental cream, washing your lives with pity, smoothing your ways with vague apologies;

Pray the Men of Mars to descend upon you. Pray Jehovah to send his prophets before the avenging fire. Pray for second sight and the inner ear. Pray for bulwark against poaching patterns of dislocated days; pray for buttressing iron against insidious termite and beetle and locust and flies and lice and moth and rust and mold.

JAY WRIGHT
[1935–]

attended the University of New Mexico, the University of California at Berkeley, Union Theological Seminary in New York, and Rutgers University.

I have no statement to make about poetry or its future.

The Charge

I

This is the morning.
There is a boy,
riding the shadow of a cradle,
clapping from room to room
as swift as the memory of him.
But it is no memory.
I did not come at this hour.
And if I had,
and if I were a memory,
would I be here now,
fully awake,
as sure of your memory
as of myself
who would be your memory?
These sounds, this image,
are not memory,
but the heart's throb past all defeats,
a livable assertion.
Now,
I hear you whistle through the house,
pushing wheels, igniting fires,
leaving no sound untried,
no room in which a young boy,
at sea in a phantom cradle,
could lurch and scream
and come to settle in the house.
You are so volubly alone,
that I turn,
reaching into the light for the boy
your father charged you to deliver.

II

We stand, and watch
my young wife's body rise and fall.
We wait to release ourselves
with the cry that makes the moon sway.
Soon,
there will be dancing,
a slow retreat to the water,
where women will hold the boy
plucked from the weeds,
a manchild, discovered,
waiting.
That is the memory
that will begin it,
an unconscious possession
of what coming like rain,
and the image of rain, can mean.

III

Now, father,
I am yours again,
and you belong to him
and the father who charged you.
But it isn't true yet.
I have only been dreaming,
and caught in the dream
of bringing him here,
where what is given
is only a memory,
and still no memory,
where death is all I have
to offer him,
though I go on living,

drawing closer, as I age, to you.
Even in this dream,
I call you to come to him.
Even though this is no more than a dream,
I call you to argue him
into existence.
No,
no word is enough.
Even the image will not come again,
unless I give it my assent.

IV

Careful in everything,
we have prepared a place,
just at that spot
where the sun forever enters this circle.
Fathers and sons sit,
making the noise of fathers,
waiting for the cut
into the life of my son,
waiting for my modest life
to be as whole as theirs.
All things here move
with that global rhythm.
All memories come
after the heat of it.
We are petals,
closed at evening,
opening at the first touch.
We are gathered to watch
the shaping of another miracle.
We are gathered in the miracle
of our own memories.

Unhappy sun,
even you cannot light everything.

V

This is the morning
when I am fully awake
to your sadness.
Now, father,
I am more than yours,
and lead you past the tricks
of our memory,
into this moment
as real as memory.
This is the moment
when all our unwelcome deaths
charge us to be free.
And my late son,
no savior,
rises still to fill
our vacant eyes.

Altars and Sacrifice

I

Even this is movement.
I see each point and body change,
and come again.
They move as my eyes would have them,
yet move and change as the light,
as the word, direct them.
On that point of the world,
the blood divides,
caught by the god,
caught in the crucible
of the victim's life,
where the word will return.
I have asked you to choose me,
knowing myself impure,
neither living nor dead.
Arrogant like this,
I have begun to design
my own god.
Arrogant like this,
I am sure of the perfect
divination,
the release from myself,
into the words you cannot say,
into the act you cannot perform.
Surely, I can argue
that something has been lost.
Surely, my father
will make me an infant again,
casting for my name,
consecrating my newborn altar,

stringing the god's teeth
on a necklace around my neck.
But how will I stand?
Am I the babe or the vicar
of the god?
This morning, it is clear,
the divination tosses me back.
I stand,
not wholly lost,
not fully chosen,
and watch the act played out.

II

It should be winter here.
It should be time
for the warmth of blood,
for the warmth of the breath,
to enter and contain us.
This incomplete one
has been chosen again.
Above him,
God's vicar sits like the rain,
and sends his messenger to earth,
into these shadows,
with the instrument
as sharp as God's teeth,
with a need like ours.
Half-man, half-woman,
the victim will stand,
his eyes fixed
on the suffering of the world,
to be split from navel through sex.
When it is done,

the incomplete one will take
the crucible of the word into himself,
speaking, to release that greater part
for which we wait.
Now, the God will turn
this blood into stars,
beginning that small movement again,
moving again into the memory
of his first gift,
his first destruction,
moving again
toward that first naming,
that first delegation of powers.

III

You wear, I know,
these emblems now,
these covenant stones to design
your own prefiguration.
Even when the Fox steps
in your most secret corners,
even when the seed
is threatened by his step,
you parcel out the word,
the resurrection,
without mourning.
In God's winding,
in his center,
I learn of the movement of stars,
of time and seasons,
learn how to inhabit this space.
This broken body fills again
with the memory of fathers,

their slow recovery,
my slow movement
into this ordered world.
Father, standing here,
watching this broken and fulfilled design,
I find my arrogant impurity
shaking to the kɔ kɔ kɔ
and the rhythm of the smith.

The Dead

The dance grows
from the sleeping eye,
the image of death.
I see the Fox,
creeping into God's chamber,
ignorant of death,
believing his father dead.
I see the God himself, dancing,
turning about himself
like the stars he moves,
turning into himself
like the dead he caresses.
Still, my dead go rootless,
without names,
without altar-pots.
Often, I frighten myself,
listening, here in the courtyard,
in your silences,
for a flutter,
a sign, in your hesitation,
in the movement of your hand.
At night,
I hear you call,
and snap myself awake,
and tell myself it isn't time,
that you wouldn't leave me
here at the entrance,
hardly able to speak the names
of those who return,
out of season, with you,

by night.
No, I will not face it,
though I know that even
the god died unfinished,
yet he moves still
in the shape of the Sigui,
moves still
when we stumble in drink,
the living dead.
But it is not enough
to sip the knowledge
of our failings.
The masks dance
on this small point, leading
this soul, these souls,
into the rhythm
of the eye stripped of sight,
the hand stripped of touch,
the heart stripped of love,
the body stripped of its own beginning,
into the rhythm
of emptiness and return,
into the self
moving against itself,
into the self
moving into itself,
the word, and the first design.
Now,
I designate myself your child,
nanī I can name,
and see this fire, burning between us,
moving like water,
caressing these birds,
these stones,

your sandalled feet,
and the sound of your voice.
All these will have their place,
twin and totem,
earth and warrior.
All these will gather at my dama.
I sit here with you,
and my hands learn the feel
of cloth and seeds and earth again.
I trade these cowries.
I learn these relations.
This is the moment
when all our unwelcome deaths
charge us to be free.
And I wear these covenant stones,
a sign,
that your world moves still.